LOW TYRAMINE COOKBOOK

MAIN COURSE – 80 + Low-Tyramine Breakfast, Main Course, Dessert and Snacks Recipes

TABLE OF CONTENTS

Introduction

Low tyramine recipes for personal enjoyment but also for family enjoyment. You will love them for sure for how easy it is to prepare them.

PUMPKIN CUPCAKES

Serves: **4**

Prep Time: **10** Minutes

Cook Time: **30** Minutes

Total Time: **40** Minutes

INGREDIENTS

- 1 cup pumpkin puree
- 1 tsp cinnamon
- ½ tsp mixed spice
- 1 tsp ginger
- ¼ lb. butter
- 1 cups brown sugar
- 2 eggs
- 2 cups flour
- 3 tsp baking powder

DIRECTIONS

1. Boil the pumpkin and then puree in a food processor
2. Cream butter and sugar, add the eggs and beat well, stir in pureed pumpkin and dry ingredients
3. Combine all ingredients and spoon mixture into a muffin tin
4. Bake at 300 F for 20 minutes, remove and serve

Serves: **2**

Prep Time: **10**   Minutes

Cook Time: **10**   Minutes

Total Time: **20**   Minutes

INGREDIENTS

- 1 cup buckwheat mix
- 1 egg
- 1 cup milk
- 1 tablespoon butter

DIRECTIONS

1. In a bow mix all ingredients, add olive oil and pour batter
2. Cook for 1-2 minutes per side
3. Remove and serve

CARROT CAKE

Serves: **4**

Prep Time: **10**   Minutes

Cook Time: **40**   Minutes

Total Time: **50**   Minutes

INGREDIENTS

- 1 cup whole meal self raising flour
- 1 cup brown sugar
- 1 cup self raising flour
- 1 tsp salt
- 1 tsp cinnamon
- 1 tsp ginger
- 1 cup olive oil
- 2 cups carrots
- 3 eggs
- ½ tsp allspice

DIRECTIONS

1. Preheat oven to 275 F and place all ingredients in a bowl except eggs
2. In another bowl mix eggs and add to the mixture
3. Pour into cake in
4. For carrot cake pour batter into cupcake molds
5. Bake for 40 minutes
6. Remove and serve

RUSSIAN FUDGE

Serves: 2

Prep Time: *10* Minutes

Cook Time: *30* Minutes

Total Time: *40* Minutes

INGREDIENTS

- ½ butter
- 1 can condensed milk
- ¾ cup milk
- 2 tablespoons golden syrup
- 3 cups sugar
- 1 tablespoon vanilla essence

DIRECTIONS

1. **In a pot place all the ingredients except vanilla essence and bring to boil**
2. **Boil for 15-20 minutes and in another bowl drop some fudge mixture**
3. **Add vanilla essence and beat with a mixer for 5-6 minutes**

4. Pour into greased tin and place in fridge
5. Cut into pieces and serve

GINGER BEER

Serves: **2**

Prep Time: **10** Minutes

Cook Time: **20** Minutes

Total Time: **30** Minutes

INGREDIENTS

- 1-inch ginger
- 4 tablespoons brown sugar
- 1 tsp citric acid
- 1 L soda water
- fresh mint

DIRECTIONS

1. **Grate ginger and mix with the rest of ingredients and let them sit for 10-12 minutes**
2. **Serve when ready**

CINNAMON SCONES

Serves: **4**

Prep Time: **10**   Minutes

Cook Time: **30**   Minutes

Total Time: **40**   Minutes

INGREDIENTS

- 2 cups self raising flour
- 2 tablespoons butter
- 2/3 cups milk

FILLING

- 1/3 cup butter
- ¾ cup brown sugar
- 1 tsp cinnamon

DIRECTIONS

1. Preheat oven to 350 F
2. In a blender add butter, flour and blend until smooth
3. Add milk and blend or another 1-2 minutes

4. Remove mixture onto floured surface
5. In the blender put all ingredients for the filling and blend until smooth
6. Spread the filling into the dough

MAC AND CHEESELESS

Serves: *4*

Prep Time: *10*   Minutes

Cook Time: *30*   Minutes

Total Time: *40*   Minutes

INGREDIENTS

- 1 leek
- 1 clove garlic
- sat
- citric acid
- 1 tsp turmeric
- 1 tsp cumin
- 1 tsp coriander powder
- ½ cup roasted sunflower seeds
- 1 tablespoon rice flour
- 1 tsp arrowroot
- 1 cup broccoli
- 2 tablespoons butter
- 1 cup milk
- macaroni pasta

DIRECTIONS

1. Cook pasta, add leek and sauté with butter, citric acid and pepper
2. Add butter, cumin, coriander powder, turmeric, sunflower seeds
3. Add arrowroot and rice flour and cook for 2-3 minutes
4. Add broccoli, pasta and stir
5. Cook for 20 minutes at 350 F, remove and serve

Serves: **4**

Prep Time: **10**   Minutes

Cook Time: **20**   Minutes

Total Time: **30**   Minutes

INGREDIENTS

- rice noodles
- onion
- cucumber
- carrot
- Coriander
- zucchini
- carrot
- Thai mint
- Chives
- Roasted sunflower seeds
- ginger
- rice paper
- tofu

DIRECTIONS

1. In a bowl place the noodles and boil, cover with a lid
2. When they are cool set aside, soak a couple of rice papers in warm water and place the rice paper on a towel
3. Place the noodles and the rest of rest of ingredients on a rice paper and fold
4. Serve when ready

GINGER CRUNCH

Serves: **4**

Prep Time: **10**   Minutes

Cook Time: **30**   Minutes

Total Time: **40**   Minutes

INGREDIENTS

-   ¼ lb. butter
-   ½ cup sugar
-   1 cup plain flour
-   ½ whole meal flour
-   1 tsp baking powder
-   1 tsp ginger

DIRECTIONS

1. In a food processor add butter and soon and blend until smooth
2. Add the rest of ingredients and blend
3. Remove from blender and bake for 20 minutes at 350 F

4. Cut into cookie shape and serve

Serves: **2**

Prep Time: **10**   Minutes

Cook Time: **10**   Minutes

Total Time: **20**   Minutes

INGREDIENTS

- 1 cup corn flour
- 1 egg
- 1 cup milk
- 1 tablespoon butter
- 2 tablespoons honey
- ½ cup rice flour
- 1 tsp baking powder
- ½ tsp salt

DIRECTIONS

1. Let sit for 8-10 minutes
2. Place in the waffle iron and cook
3. Remove and serve

CHEESE CAKE

Serves: **4**

Prep Time: **10**   Minutes

Cook Time: **30**   Minutes

Total Time: **40**   Minutes

INGREDIENTS

- ½ lb. gingernut biscuits
- ½ lb. blueberries
- 1 tsp vanilla extract
- 1 tsp acid
- ¼ lb. butter
- ¼ lb. caster sugar
- 2 tablespoons arrowroot
- ¼ lb. full-fat Philadelphia
- 2 eggs

DIRECTIONS

1. Preheat oven to 350 F

2. In a bowl mix butter and biscuits and press into the base of the tin
3. Bake for 10-12 minutes
4. In a saucepan cook blueberry with sugar and milk for 10-12 minutes
5. Take off heat add citric acid and vanilla
6. Bake for 40 minutes remove and let it chill

BASIC WAFFLES

Serves: *2*
Prep Time: *10* Minutes

Cook Time: *10* Minutes

Total Time: *20* Minutes

INGREDIENTS

- 2 eggs
- 1 tablespoon sugar
- 1 tablespoon baking powder
- 1 cup flour
- 1/8 cup milk
- ½ tsp vanilla essence

DIRECTIONS

1. In a food processor add all the ingredients and blend until smooth
2. Heat the waffle iron pour in the batter
3. Cook until golden
4. Serve with maple syrup

Serves: **4**

Prep Time: **10** Minutes

Cook Time: **20** Minutes

Total Time: **30** Minutes

INGREDIENTS

- 1 tablespoon olive oil
- 4 tablespoons popcorn kernels

CARAMEL SAUCE

- 1 tablespoon butter
- 1 tablespoon brown sugar
- 1 tablespoon golden syrup

DIRECTIONS

1. In a saucepan pour olive oil and popcorn kernels over medium heat and cover
2. Shake the saucepan to distribute evenly
3. In another saucepan melt the caramel sauce ingredients

4. Remove from heat and pour over your popcorn

Serves: **4**

Prep Time: **10** Minutes

Cook Time: **10** Minutes

Total Time: **20** Minutes

INGREDIENTS

- ½ tsp salt
- 1 cup plain flour
- 1 tsp olive oil
- 1 onion
- ½ cup hot water
- 1 tablespoon cold water

DIRECTIONS

1. In a bowl mix all ingredients
2. Pour mixture into a pan and cook for 1-2 minutes per side
3. Remove and serve

TOASTED MUESLI

Serves: **4**

Prep Time: **10**   Minutes

Cook Time: **60**   Minutes

Total Time: **70**   Minutes

INGREDIENTS

- 2 cups oats
- 1 cup oat mix
- ½ cup sunflower seeds
- ½ cup sunflower oil

DIRECTIONS

1. In a bowl mix all ingredients
2. Bake for 60 minutes at 275 F
3. Garnish with blueberries and serve

Serves: **4**

Prep Time: **10**   Minutes

Cook Time: **30**   Minutes

Total Time: **40**   Minutes

INGREDIENTS

- 2 oz. butter
- 1 cup self raising flour
- ½ tsp salt
- 3 tablespoons ginger
- ½ cup milk
- 1 egg beaten
- 1 tablespoons vanilla extract
- ½ cup golden syrup
- ½ cup maple syrup
- ½ cup honey

DIRECTIONS

1. **Preheat oven to 300 F**

2. In a pan melt honey, butter, syrup and set aside

3. White syrup mixture is cooling, grate the ginger and add to the syrup mixture

4. Add flour, salt, milk, egg and vanilla extract

5. Form small cookies and bake for 15-18 minutes at 300 F

6. Remove and serve

VANILLA CHIA PUDDING

Serves: **4**

Prep Time: **10**   Minutes

Cook Time: **10**   Minutes

Total Time: **20**   Minutes

INGREDIENTS

- 2 cups hemp milk
- 2 packets stevia
- ½ tsp cinnamon
- ½ cup chia seeds
- 1 tablespoon vanilla extract

DIRECTIONS

1. **In a bowl whisk all ingredients together**
2. **Let it chill overnight and serve**

Serves: **6**

Prep Time: **10**   Minutes

Cook Time: **10**   Minutes

Total Time: **20**   Minutes

INGREDIENTS

- **12 oz. coconut milk**
- **½ cup rum**
- **2 eggs**
- **¼ tsp nutmeg**
- **¼ cup organic coconut sugar**

DIRECTIONS

1. **Blend all ingredients until smooth**
2. **Store in jar and serve with grated nutmeg**

STRAWBERRY CREAM CAKE

Serves: **8**

Prep Time: **10** Minutes

Cook Time: **30** Minutes

Total Time: **40** Minutes

INGREDIENTS

- 2 batches coconut whipped cream
- 1 pint strawberries
- 1 package fresh mint leaves
- 2 boxes Pamela's Honey Grahams

DIRECTIONS

1. Prepare coconut whipped cream according to the indications
2. Spread a layer of whipped cream on your cake place
3. Arrange grahams on top, spread a layer of coconut whipped cream and then strawberries
4. Top with mint leaves, refrigerate for 8-9 hours and serve

STRAWBERRIES AND CREAM POPS

Serves: *8*
Prep Time: *10*   Minutes

Cook Time: *20*   Minutes

Total Time: *30*   Minutes

INGREDIENTS

- 2 cups coconut milk
- 20 drops organic stevia
- 2 cups starberries
- 1 tablespoon vanilla extract

DIRECTIONS

1. In a blender blend vanilla extract, stevia and coconut milk until smooth
2. Pour 1/3 of the mixture in a glass and refrigerate
3. Add strawberries to the blender and blend
4. Fill the popsicle molds with 1/3 with the strawberry mixture and freeze for 50-60 minutes
5. Add coconut milk mixture to each mold, filling 2/3 and tp with strawberry

6. Freeze for 30-40 minutes
7. Insert the sticks and return to freezer
8. When ready remove and serve

PEAR-PECAN CARAMEL SAUCE

Serves: **6**

Prep Time: **10** Minutes

Cook Time: **10** Minutes

Total Time: **20** Minutes

INGREDIENTS

- 2 tablespoons butter
- 2 tablespoons coconut sugar
- ½ tsp cinnamon
- ½ cup pecans
- 3 pears
- ½ cup apple rum

DIRECTIONS

1. Place butter in a skillet over medium heat and cover with a lid
2. Add sugar, cinnamon and mix
3. Add pears, pecan to the pan and stir
4. Cook until pears are soft

5. In a bowl microwave rum

6. Pour the rum over pear mixture, cover and cook for 1-2 minutes

7. When ready, remove from heat and serve

MAIN DISHES

GRAIN FREE PASTA SALAD

Serves: **6**

Prep Time: **10**   Minutes

Cook Time: **10**   Minutes

Total Time: **20**   Minutes

INGREDIENTS

- 10 oz. red lentil pasta
- ½ tsp salt
- 1 tsp black pepper
- 1 package basil leaves
- 1 package oregano leaves
- 1 zucchini
- 6 oz. mushrooms
- 2 tablespoons olive oil
- 10 oz. red pepper

DIRECTIONS

1. Cook pasta according to package directions
2. Preheat oven to 425 F
3. In vegetables on a baking sheet and drizzle olive oil and toss well
4. Roast for 10-12 minutes or until golden brown
5. Remove and add basil leaves and oregano leaves

Serves: *2*
Prep Time: *10*   Minutes

Cook Time: *10*   Minutes

Total Time: *20*   Minutes

INGREDIENTS

- 2 bunches parsley
- 1 lemon
- 2 green onions
- 12 oz. cheery tomatoes
- 1 cucumber
- 1 tablespoon olive oil
- ½ tsp black pepper
- ½ tsp salt
- 1 bunch mint leaves
- 5 oz. hemp seeds

DIRECTIONS

1. In a blender add parsley and mint leaves, blend until smooth
2. Add tomatoes and blend again
3. Add the remaining ingredients and blend
4. Remove and serve

Serves: **4**
Prep Time: **10** Minutes

Cook Time: **10** Minutes

Total Time: **20** Minutes

INGREDIENTS

- 6 oz. asparagus spears
- ½ tsp salt
- 1 cup coconut milk
- ½ cup cashew cream
- ½ tsp white pepper

DIRECTIONS

1. Cut asparagus in half
2. In a pot add water, asparagus and bring to boil, pour into a strainer and rinse with cold water
3. Place all the ingredients in a blender with asparagus pieces and blend until smooth
4. Warm in a microwave until hot and serve

RICE AND CARROTS

Serves: *4*

Prep Time: *10*   Minutes

Cook Time: *50*   Minutes

Total Time: *60*   Minutes

INGREDIENTS

- 1 handful parsley
- 1 cup wild rice
- 2 ribs celery
- ½ black pepper
- 1 tablespoon olive oil
- 1 carrot

DIRECTIONS

1. In a saucepan add rice and bring to boil on low heat for 40 minutes
2. In a skillet heat olive oil over medium heat, add celery, carrot and cook for 5-6 minutes or until tender

3. Stir in pepper, parsley, rice and cook for 2-3
    minutes
4. Remove and serve

OMELETTE

Serves: **4**

Prep Time: **10** Minutes

Cook Time: **30** Minutes

Total Time: **40** Minutes

INGREDIENTS

- 2 tablespoons butter
- 2 eggs
- ½ cup rice milk
- 2 slices American cheese

DIRECTIONS

1. In a bowl mix rice milk with eggs, whisk for 1-2 minutes and pour into a frying pan
2. Cook on each side for 2-3 minutes
3. Remove and serve with salt and pepper

TYRAMINE PIE

Serves: **4**

Prep Time: **10**   Minutes

Cook Time: **30**   Minutes

Total Time: **40**   Minutes

INGREDIENTS

- 1 ½ lb. ground lamb
- 1 onion
- ½ cup peas
- 1 bay leaf
- 1 tablespoon sugar
- 1 can chopped tomatoes
- 1 carrot
- 1 tsp flour
- 2 cloves garlic

TOPPING

- 2 potatoes
- 1 egg
- 1 drizzle olive oil
- 1 pat butter

DIRECTIONS

1. In a bowl mix rice milk with eggs
2. In a pan fry garlic and onions, add lamb, tomatoes, peas, sugar, flour, carrots and bay leaf
3. Simmer for an hour, remove and scoop mixture into casserole dish
4. Boil potatoes and place them in a bowl
5. Scoop potatoes over meat mixture and place in oven for 25 minutes at 300 F, remove and serve

Serves: **4**
Prep Time: **10** Minutes

Cook Time: **60** Minutes

Total Time: **70** Minutes

INGREDIENTS

- 1 lb. matzoh farfel
- ½ lb. butter
- 1 can peaches
- 6 eggs
- 1 tablespoon vanilla
- 2/4 tsp salt
- 1 cup sugar
- cinnamon

DIRECTIONS

1. Preheat oven at 350 F
2. Place farfel in a strainer and pour hot over, transfer to a mixing bowl

3. Beat eggs and add to farfel

4. Add juice rom canned peaches and pour mixture into a baking dish and top with peaches

5. Add remaining farfel and sprinkle with cinnamon

6. Bake for 60 minutes at 350 F

7. Remove and serve

Serves: **4**

Prep Time: **10**   Minutes

Cook Time: **60**   Minutes

Total Time: **70**   Minutes

INGREDIENTS

- 1 acorn squash
- 1 butternut squash
- 3 pats butter
- 3 tsp brown sugar

DIRECTIONS

1. Cut butternut squash and acorn lengthwise in half
2. Fill each half with 1 pat of butter and 1 tsp of sugar
3. Bake for 60 minutes at 350 F or until done,
4. Remove and dig out squash meat
5. Scoop mashed squash into a bowl and enjoy

CHICKEN POT PIE CASSEROLE

Serves: **4**

Prep Time: **10**   Minutes

Cook Time: **30**   Minutes

Total Time: **40**   Minutes

INGREDIENTS

- 2 tablespoons butter
- 2 cups vegetable stock
- 1 cooked chicken breasts
- 1 cup carrots
- 2 fresh eggs
- 2 tablespoons flour
- 1 cup zucchini
- 2 small potatoes
- 1 cup rice milk
- 1 cup Bisquick

DIRECTIONS

1. In a saucepan melt butter on low heat

2. Add flour, vegetable stock and stir
3. Bring to boil and add carrots, potatoes, onion, chicken, zucchini
4. Mix well and reduce heat, simmer for 5-6 minutes, season with salt
5. Pour mixture into a baking dish and set aside
6. In a bowl mix rice milk, eggs and Bisquick, pour mixture Bisquick over mixture
7. Bake at 375 F for 25 minutes remove and serve

Serves: **4**

Prep Time: **10** Minutes

Cook Time: **30** Minutes

Total Time: **40** Minutes

INGREDIENTS

- 2 tablespoons butter
- 1 lb. salmon
- 1 onion
- 1 cup Italian rice
- 2 cups boiling homemade vegetable stock
- 1 yellow zucchini

DIRECTIONS

1. In a cooking pot place butter and cook on medium heat
2. Stir in zucchini, onions and cook for 30 minutes, add rice, pour boiling stock and cover for another 40 minutes

3. Stir in the salmon into the risotto and season with salt

4. Cook until the rice is tender, remove from slow cooker

5. Spoon into a plate and serve!

CAROB BUTTER

Serves: *8*

Prep Time: *10*   Minutes

Cook Time: *20*   Minutes

Total Time: *30*   Minutes

INGREDIENTS

- 1 cup sunflower seeds
- ½ cup carob powder
- 3 tablespoons coconut oil
- 1 cup hem seeds
- 30 drops stevia

DIRECTIONS

1. Preheat oven to 275 F
2. Place sunflower seeds on baking sheets
3. Bake seeds for 8-10 minutes or until golden brown
4. Place the seeds and stevia in a blender and blend until smooth

5. Blend carob powder in another bowl and add to the blender

6. Blend them together and pour in jar and store in the refrigerator

Serves: **6**

Prep Time: **10**   Minutes

Cook Time: **40**   Minutes

Total Time: **50**   Minutes

INGREDIENTS

- 1 tablespoon olive oil
- 1 cup sweet potatoes
- 1 cup potatoes
- 1 cup celery
- ¾ cup carrots
- 1 cup peas
- 6 oz. tempeh firm tofu
- 1 cup mushrooms soup
- 1 gluten-free pie crust
- 1 cup onions

DIRECTIONS

1. **Preheat oven to 325 F**

2. Place a pan over medium heat, add onion, oil and veggies
3. Cook until golden brown
4. Cut tofu into small cubes, stir in potatoes, peas, tofu, and stir
5. Lay mixture over pie crust and bake for 30-35 minutes or until golden brown
6. Remove and serve

Serves: **4**

Prep Time: **10**   Minutes

Cook Time: **30**   Minutes

Total Time: **40**   Minutes

INGREDIENTS

- 1 onion
- ½ tsp mustard seeds
- ½ tsp cardamom seeds
- 5 cups vegetable stock
- 5 cups kale
- 2 cups peas
- 1 clove garlic
- 1 tablespoon curry powder
- 1 tsp cumin seeds
- 1 tsp coriander seeds
- 1 tsp coconut sugar

DIRECTIONS

1. Chop kale into 1-inch pieces
2. Mince the garlic clove and dice the onion, slice them into small slices
3. In a skillet toast the spices over medium heat
4. In a soup pot heat olive oil, add onion, garlic and the toasted spiced and cook for 2-3 minutes
5. Add broth, tomatoes, kale, peas and stir to combine
6. Bring to boil, and simmer on low heat
7. Cook for 1-2 hours add salt and serve

VEGGIE SOUP

Serves: **6**

Prep Time: **10** Minutes

Cook Time: **30** Minutes

Total Time: **40** Minutes

INGREDIENTS

- 3 zucchini
- 2 celery stalks
- 1 lb. green beans
- 1 bunch parsley
- 4 kale leaves
- 3 green onions
- 2 tomatoes
- 2 clove garlic
- 2 tablespoons coconut aminos
- 1 avocado
- 2 carrots
- 1 handful cilantro
- 2 tablespoons teff seeds
- 2 tablespoons seaweed flakes

DIRECTIONS

1. Prepare the veggies and place them in a blender, blend until smooth
2. Add mixture to a stock pot, add water, teff, seaweed and bring to boil, simmer on low heat for 25-30 minutes
3. Remove and serve

Serves: **4**

Prep Time: **10** Minutes

Cook Time: **30** Minutes

Total Time: **40** Minutes

INGREDIENTS

- 2 tablespoons olive oil
- 1 tablespoon lemon juice
- 1 tablespoon curry powder
- ½ tsp salt
- ½ tsp paprika
- ½ tsp chipotle powder
- 1 head cauliflower

DIRECTIONS

1. Preheat oven to 325 F
2. Wash the cauliflower and remove the leaves
3. Cut the cauliflower into 1-inch pieces

4. In a bowl mix pepper, oil, lemon juice, salt and curry powder

5. Add cauliflower slices and toss to coat

6. Spread vegetables in a single layer in a baking pan and bake for 30 minutes or until brown

7. Remove and serve

Serves: **1**

Prep Time: **10**   Minutes

Cook Time: **120**   Minutes

Total Time: **130**   Minutes

INGREDIENTS

- 1 egg
- 1 egg yolk
- 1 cup live oil
- 1 tablespoon apple cider vinegar
- ½ tsp mustard
- ½ sea salt
- ½ tsp tartar

DIRECTIONS

1. In a bowl mix all the ingredients and pour into a blender, blend until smooth
2. Remove and store in a jar

PALEO RICE

Serves: **6**

Prep Time: **10** Minutes

Cook Time: **40** Minutes

Total Time: **50** Minutes

INGREDIENTS

- 2 tablespoons olive oil
- 12 oz. kale
- 2 tablespoons cilantro
- ½ cup chicken stock
- 1 cup celery
- 2 cloves garlic
- 2 bell peppers
- 12 oz. turkey
- 2 cups cauliflower rice

DIRECTIONS

1. **In a Dutch oven heat oil over medium heat**

2. Sauté the the celery for 4-5 minutes, add bell peppers, garlic and cook for 2-3 minutes

3. Add turkey and the remaining ingredients and cook for 25-30 minutes

4. Remove and serve

LANGOSTINO CHOWDER

Serves: **6**

Prep Time: **10**   Minutes

Cook Time: **30**   Minutes

Total Time: **40**   Minutes

INGREDIENTS

- 1 pinch saffron
- 12 oz. langoustine tails
- 1/2cup hot water
- 1 cup coconut milk
- ½ tsp white pepper
- ¼ tsp salt
- 1 bell pepper
- 1 cup corn
- 12 oz. potatoes

DIRECTIONS

1. Place the saffron into the hot water, add coconut milk, corn, roasted pepper

2. Blend until smooth, place the ingredients without langoustine into a saucepan, bring to boil

3. Reduce heat and simmer for 15-20 minutes

4. Stir in langoustine and cook for 5-6 minutes, top with parsley and serve

CURRIED CHICKEN SALAD

Serves: **4**

Prep Time: **10** Minutes

Cook Time: **30** Minutes

Total Time: **40** Minutes

INGREDIENTS

- 5 tablespoons mayonnaise
- 1 tsp curry powder
- 10 oz. chicken breast
- 1 apple
- 1 stalk celery
- ½ cup pecans

DIRECTIONS

1. In a bowl mix all salad ingredients
2. Serve with lettuce or baby arugula

Serves: **4**

Prep Time: **10**   Minutes

Cook Time: **30**   Minutes

Total Time: **40**   Minutes

INGREDIENTS

- 1 cup carrots
- 1 radish
- ½ cup celery
- ½ cup zucchini

LEFTOVERS DRESSING

- 1 tablespoon mustard
- 2 tablespoons olive oil
- 1 tablespoon apple cider vinegar

DIRECTIONS

1. Slice vegetables and mix in a bowl
2. In another bowl prepare dressing and pour over salad, serve when ready

WHITE BEAN AND TOMATO SALAD

Serves: **6**
Prep Time: **10**   Minutes

Cook Time: **10**   Minutes

Total Time: **20**   Minutes

INGREDIENTS

- 2 15 oz. cans white kidney beans
- 2/3 cup red onion
- ½ cup fresh dill
- 2 tablespoons lemon juice
- 1 tablespoon white vinegar
- 2 garlic cloves
- 2 halved grape tomatoes
- ¼ cup olive oil

DIRECTIONS

1. In a bowl toss all ingredients and season with salt
2. Let it marinade as long as you wish and serve

Serves: 2
Prep Time: *10*   Minutes

Cook Time: *50*   Minutes

Total Time: *60*   Minutes

INGREDIENTS

- 2 russet potato
- olive oil
- salt
- red pepper
- garlic powder
- oregano
- basil

DIRECTIONS

1. Wedge potatoes into 6-8 pieces
2. Drizzle with olive oil and season with salt
3. Add red pepper, basil, oregano and garlic powder
4. Bake at 375 F for 45 minutes, remove and serve

Serves: *3*

Prep Time: *10*   Minutes

Cook Time: *40*   Minutes

Total Time: *50*   Minutes

INGREDIENTS

- 1 lb. elbow macaroni
- 3 tablespoons olive oil
- salt
- ½ tsp salt

DIRECTIONS

1. In a saucepan boil water and add macaroni, olive oil and salt, boil for 8-10 minutes
2. In a frying pan add olive oil over medium heat, add macaroni, salt and pepper
3. Cook for about 25-30 minutes, transfer to a bowl, top with ketchup and serve with roast beef

MASHED POTATOES

Serves: **2**

Prep Time: **10**   Minutes

Cook Time: **20**   Minutes

Total Time: **30**   Minutes

INGREDIENTS

- 2 russet potatoes
- 2 tablespoons butter
- 1 tsp salt
- 1 cup milk

DIRECTIONS

1. Cut potatoes and place them in a pan with water
2. Bring to boil and simmer for 15-20 minutes
3. Drain water and add salt, butter, mash the potatoes
4. Add ½ milk and continue to mash, add the remaining milk and mix well
5. Serve when ready

Serves: **4**

Prep Time: **10** Minutes

Cook Time: **30** Minutes

Total Time: **40** Minutes

INGREDIENTS

- 1 tsp apple cider vinegar
- 2 tablespoons sugar
- ½ tsp cinnamon
- 1-gallon water
- 6 large apples
- 3 granny smith apples

DIRECTIONS

1. In a bowl mix water and vinegar, add peeled apples into vinegar and remove when they are ready
2. Place in a slow cooker with sugar and cook for 6-7 hours on low heat or until tender
3. Add cinnamon, remaining sugar and serve

Serves: **4**

Prep Time: **10**   Minutes

Cook Time: **10**   Minutes

Total Time: **20**   Minutes

INGREDIENTS

- ½ cup dried tomatoes
- ½ cup olive oil
- 1 tablespoon lemon juice
- salt, pepper
- 1 lb. cubed potatoes
- 1 cup scallions
- ½ tsp cumin

DIRECTIONS

1. Cut potatoes into ½ inch cubes and place in a saucepan with salted water
2. Cover pan and bring to boil, simmer on low heat

3. In a bowl add scallions, olive oil, lemon juice and cumin

4. Drain the tomatoes and squeeze them, chop them and add them to the bowl

5. Add potatoes to the salad and toss well

6. Add salt and serve

GREEN PEPPER SALAD

Serves: **4**

Prep Time: **10** Minutes

Cook Time: **10** Minutes

Total Time: **20** Minutes

INGREDIENTS

- 3 green bell peppers
- 4 poblano peppers
- 2 tomatoes
- ½ onion
- 2 tablespoons cilantro
- ½ tsp cumin
- 2 tablespoons olive oil
- 2 tablespoons lemon juice
- black pepper

DIRECTIONS

1. Grill the peppers for 2-3 minutes per side

2. In a bowl add grilled peppers and the rest of the ingredients

3. Season with salt and serve

OVEN BAKED POLENTA

Serves: *4*

Prep Time: *10*   Minutes

Cook Time: *30*   Minutes

Total Time: *40*   Minutes

INGREDIENTS

- ¾ cornmeal
- 1 tsp marjoram
- salt
- pepper
- ½ cup milk
- 2 tablespoons butter

DIRECTIONS

1. Preheat oven to 400 F
2. In a baking dish whisk cornmeal, salt, pepper and water
3. Cover and bake for 30-35 minute

4. Remove from the oven, add butter, marjoram and milk

5. Whisk until smooth and serve

Serves: **4**

Prep Time: **15**   Minutes

Cook Time: **40**   Minutes

Total Time: **55**   Minutes

INGREDIENTS

- 2 cup strawberries
- 2 cup rhubarb
- 1 cup sugar
- 5 tablespoons tapioca
- ½ tsp
- ½ tsp nutmeg
- 2 refrigerated pie crusts

DIRECTIONS

1. In a bowl mix all ingredients and cover for 15-20 minutes
2. Line a pie plate with one of the pastries and fill with fruit mixture

3. Bake at 375 for 40 minute or until done
4. Remove and serve

STRAWBERRY ICE-CREAM

Serves: **4**

Prep Time: **10**   Minutes

Cook Time: **30**   Minutes

Total Time: **40**   Minutes

INGREDIENTS

- ¾ cup sugar
- 1 tablespoon cornstarch
- 1 cup milk
- ¾ cup whipping cream
- 2 sliced strawberries
- 2 tablespoons pomegranate juice

DIRECTIONS

1. In a saucepan stir sugar and cornstarch, whisk in cream and milk
2. Whisk over medium heat until base thickens, pour into bowl and cool
3. In a blender add strawberries and blend until smooth

4. Strain into ice-cream base, mix in pomegranate juice and chill for 3-4 hours

5. Process in ice-cream maker following indications and freeze

ROASTED BRUSSELS SPROUTS

Serves: *4*

Prep Time: *10*   Minutes

Cook Time: *30*   Minutes

Total Time: *40*   Minutes

INGREDIENTS

- 1 lb. of Brussels sprouts
- 3 tablespoons olive oil
- 4 cloves garlic
- salt
- 1 tablespoon white vinegar

DIRECTIONS

1. Preheat oven to 400 F
2. Trim bottom of Brussels sprouts
3. Heat oil in cast iron over medium heat and place sprouts, add garlic and salt
4. Cook until sprouts begin to brown and transfer to oven

5. Bake for 25 minutes, remove and serve

COLE SLAW

Serves: *4*

Prep Time: *10*   Minutes

Cook Time: *10*   Minutes

Total Time: *20*   Minutes

INGREDIENTS

- 1 tsp white pepper
- 1 tsp black pepper
- 1 tsp mustard
- 1 tsp salt
- 1 tsp garlic powder
- 1 tsp celery seed
- ½ cup sugar
- 2 tablespoons parsley
- 1 tsp white vinegar
- 1 cup mayonnaise
- ½ cup red cabbage
- ½ cup carrots
- 1 lb. shredded cabbage

DIRECTIONS

1. In a bowl mix all ingredients with vinegar and mayonnaise
2. Add salt and serve

Serves: **4**

Prep Time: **10** Minutes

Cook Time: **40** Minutes

Total Time: **50** Minutes

INGREDIENTS

- 2 chicken breasts
- 2 scallions
- 1 cup mayonnaise
- 2 tablespoons lemon juice
- 2 tablespoons parsley leaves
- 1 apple
- 5 tablespoons walnuts
- 1 tablespoon vegetable oil
- salt
- 2 ribs celery

DIRECTIONS

1. Bake chicken breast in the oven, remove and shred meat
2. Mix all salad ingredients with chicken and serve

CHERRY TOMATO SALAD WITH BASIL

Serves: **5**

Prep Time: **10**   Minutes

Cook Time: **30**   Minutes

Total Time: **40**   Minutes

INGREDIENTS

- 5 slices ciabatta
- 2 tablespoons olive oil
- salt
- 20 basil leaves
- 1 lemon zest
- 3 cups cherry tomatoes
- 1 lb. mozzarella balls
- ½ tsp red Chile flakes
- black pepper

DIRECTIONS

1. Preheat oven to 375 F and cut bread into small pieces, drizzle with oil and bake for 8 minutes or until golden brown

2. In a pan boil lemon zest and basil leaves, drain and transfer to a blender and blend until smooth

3. In a bowl mix mozzarella, bread cubes, cherry tomatoes, sprinkle with Chile flakes and season with salt

4. Drizzle basil oil and serve

ROASTED POTATOES

Serves: *4*

Prep Time: *10* Minutes

Cook Time: *40* Minutes

Total Time: *50* Minutes

INGREDIENTS

- ½ cup mustard
- 1 tablespoon olive oil
- 1 tablespoon butter
- 1 tablespoon lemon juice
- 2 garlic cloves
- 1 tablespoon oregano
- 1 tsp lemon peel
- 1 tsp salt
- 2 lbs. potatoes

DIRECTIONS

1. Preheat oven to 400 F

2. Whisk lemon juice, garlic, oregano, salt, olive oil, mustard, butter and blend until smooth

3. Sprinkle black pepper and toss to coat the potatoes in the mixture

4. Roast potatoes for 30-35 minutes or until golden brown

5. Remove and serve

THAI CHICKEN SALAD

Serves: **4**

Prep Time: **10** Minutes

Cook Time: **30** Minutes

Total Time: **40** Minutes

INGREDIENTS

- 2 lb. whole chicken
- ½ cup canola oil
- 2 tablespoons peanut butter
- 2 tsp brown sugar
- 1 tsp red pepper flakes
- ½ cucumber
- 1 carrot
- ½ cup lime juice
- 2 tablespoons water
- 2 cloves garlic
- 2 tsp ginger
- 3 scallions
- 2 tablespoons cilantro
- ½ cup peanuts

DIRECTIONS

1. Season chicken with salt and pepper
2. Roast at 350 F for 60 minutes
3. Shred meat from the chicken
4. Puree lime juice, water, peanut butter, salt, garlic, ginger, brown sugar and pepper flakes
5. Transfer to a bowl and refrigerate
6. Add carrot, cucumber, scallions, vinaigrette, cilantro and toss to combine
7. Add chicken and toss well
8. Season with salt, peanuts and serve

Serves: **4**

Prep Time: **10**   Minutes

Cook Time: **30**   Minutes

Total Time: **40**   Minutes

INGREDIENTS

- 3 cloves garlic
- 1-inch jalapeno pepper
- 3 potatoes
- ½ onion
- ½ green pepper
- 6 leaves cilantro
- ½ lemon juice
- 1 tsp salt

DIRECTIONS

1. **In a blender add jalapeno and garlic and blend until smooth**

2. Add remaining ingredients and serve with tortilla chips

TOMATO JAM

Serves: **4**
Prep Time: **10**   Minutes

Cook Time: **30**   Minutes

Total Time: **40**   Minutes

INGREDIENTS

- 1 tsp olive oil
- 1 garlic clove
- 2 cans diced tomatoes
- 1 tablespoon sugar
- 1 cup onion
- ½ dried thyme
- ½ tsp salt
- ½ tsp black pepper

DIRECTIONS

1. **In a saucepan heat oil over medium heat, add onion garlic and cook until soft, add tomatoes, sugar, thyme, black pepper and salt**

2. Cook on high until all liquid evaporates

3. Remove and serve

BBQ SAUCE

Serves: **4**

Prep Time: **10**   Minutes

Cook Time: **10**   Minutes

Total Time: **20**   Minutes

INGREDIENTS

- 1 cup brown sugar
- ½ cup salt
- 2 tablespoon celery seed
- 2 tablespoon cumin
- 2 tablespoon cayenne pepper
- 2 tablespoon garlic powder
- 1 tablespoon chili powder
- 2-quasts catsup
- 2 cups cider vinegar
- 1 tsp liquid smoke

DIRECTIONS

1. **In a bowl mix all spices and set aside**

2. Mix the remaining ingredients and add to the spice mixture

Serves: **4**

Prep Time: **10**   Minutes

Cook Time: **30**   Minutes

Total Time: **40**   Minutes

INGREDIENTS

- 1 lb. ground turkey
- pepper
- 2 cloves garlic
- 2 28 oz. cans tomatoes
- 1 onion
- 1 tsp fennel
- 1 tsp sugar
- 1 tsp salt
- 1 6 oz. can tomato paste
- 2 tsp oregano
- 1 tsp basil

DIRECTIONS

1. Brown the turkey in a pan, add garlic, onion and cook for another 4-5 minutes
2. Add tomato paste, tomatoes, and the rest of ingredients
3. Bring to boil and cook for 25-30 minute
4. Remove and serve

THANK YOU FOR READING THIS BOOK!

Made in the USA
Monee, IL
02 March 2021

61728463R00069